RELATIVE GENITIVE

ALSO FROM POETS & TRAITORS PRESS

Advances in Embroidery by Ahmad Al-Ashqar
Education by Windows by Johnny Lorenz

RELATIVE GENITIVE

VAL VINOKUR

poems with translations from
Osip Mandelstam & Vladimir Mayakovsky

Many of the poems and translations in this book have appeared in magazines, journals, and anthologies: "Your Worship" in *The Boston Review*; "Having Yours," "The Tristia of Count Sheremetiev II," "*Maman dlo*," and "The Book of Genesis" under different titles in *The Massachusetts Review*; "From the Other End" and "Two Packs a Day" in *New American Writing*; "A Jake's Jacket," "Getting Along with Horses," "from *About This*," "An Extraordinary Adventure...," "Letter from Paris...," in *Night Wraps the Sky: Writings by and About Mayakovsky*, edited by Michael Almereyda; and "Notre Dame" and "Leningrad," in *Osip Mandelstam: New Translations*, edited by Ilya Bernstein.

Published 2018 in New York by Poets & Traitors Press
www.poets-traitors.com
poetstraitors@gmail.com

Guest Editor: Emily Skillings
Editors: Val Vinokur, Gili Ostfield
Editorial Advisors: Stephanie Leone, Rebekah Smith, Raúl Rubio

Published in the United States of America

Poets & Traitors Press is an independent publisher of books of poetry and translations by a single author/translator. The press emerged from the Poet/Translator Reading Series and from the New School's Literary Translation Workshop to showcase authors who travel between writing and translation, artists for whom *Language* is made manifest through *languages* and whose own word carries, shapes, and is shaped by that of another.

Poets & Traitors Press acknowledges support from Melissa Friedling, Stephanie Browner, Raúl Rubio, Alex Draifinger, Jane McNamara, Eugene Lang College, the New School Bachelor's Program for Adults and Transfer Students, and the New School Foreign Languages Department.

ISBN: 978-0-9990737-1-1

Design: Gili Ostfield

for Mark Elia

CONTENTS*

*Poems by Val Vinokur are indicated as (VV), those by Osip Mandelstam as (OM), and Vladimir Mayakovsky as (VM). All translations by Val Vinokur.

Do not partake of foreign dialects, instead try best to let them pass,
For all the same your teeth will never learn to bite a piece of glass.

A flight of foreign screeching, an offering of agony—
An evil fate is what shall guard against illegal ecstasy.

Because you know: a foreign name won't save your dying heart
And your thinking and immortal mouth the moment they forever part.

And what if Tasso, Ariosto, those charmed enthrallers of our minds,
Are little more than monsters, with azure brains and scales of humid eyes?

And for your punishment, you prideful and persistent audiophile,
Accept this sponge of posca for your treasonable lips so vile.

Osip Mandelstam, May 1933 (translated by Val Vinokur)

RELATIVE
GENITIVE

FROM THE AUTHOR-TRANSLATOR

This is a picture of my son, looking at Anna Akhmatova's family photo album in her apartment-turned-museum in Petersburg on July 4, 2014. Anna's stuffed monkey sits behind him on a couch that Vladimir Mayakovsky used whenever he spent the night there, at the Fontanka House. According to the docent, the 6'2" Mayakovsky would have to remove the armrest cushions. Osip Mandelstam also sometimes spent the night on this couch, but did not need to remove the cushions in order to sleep comfortably at Anna Akhmatova's. His widow, Nadezhda Mandelstam, always objected to descriptions of him as a tiny "homeless bird." Osia was broad-shouldered, of average height, she would insist.

In the upper left corner, Pushkin gazes down from the same print that inhabited my own childhood home—first in Moscow and later in Miami Beach, packed in our bags when I arrived with my mother and grandmother in 1979. In many Soviet Jewish homes, this image took the place of icons or portraits of Lenin and rabbinic ancestors. If a self-described child of Africa could become the father of Russian literature... So went the beginning of the syllogism that had been rendered opaque in South Florida, which had its own complicated relationship to the descendants of African slaves.

This book is like Akhmatova's couch. I thought that if both Mayakovsky and Mandelstam could sleep on the same piece of furniture, then my poems could hold the space between my translations of both poets—so radically different in temperament, style, and outlook. Nadezhda Mandelstam describes how her husband became friends with Mayakovsky in Petersburg, but the two separated due to the fact that "it was 'not done' for poets of rival schools to associate with each other." Mayakovsky was a flamboyant Russian extrovert who served the Soviet regime with poster work and poetry until he could no longer muffle his more lyrical energies. Mandelstam was a refined Jewish introvert who poetically defied the regime and was killed by it. In a 1922 article on "Literary Moscow," Mandelstam writes (in Clarence Brown's translation):

> Mayakovsky is working at the elementary and enormous problem of 'poetry for everyone, not for the elite.' Of course, the extending of poetry's base proceeds at the expense of its intensity, its content, its poetic culture. Wonderfully well-informed about the wealth and complexity of world poetry, Mayakovsky, in establishing his 'poetry for everyone' has had to turn his back on whatever was incomprehensible, i.e. whatever presupposed in the listener the slightest education in poetry. But to address, in poetry, an audience totally unprepared for poetry is just as ungrateful a job as sitting on a tack. [...] But Mayakovsky writes poetry and very cultured poetry: an elegant song-and-dance man whose stanza breaks up into ponderous antitheses, is saturated with hyperbolic metaphors and sustained in monotonous accentual lines. Mayakovsky has absolutely no business impoverishing himself.

The Acmeist Mandelstam is in many ways a neo-classicist, whereas Mayakovsky is a Futurist, asking in one of his poems: "What's the point rebuilding Notre Dame?" But in Mandelstam's poem about that cathedral, it emerges that Notre Dame was never really finished in the first place. "The past has not even been born yet," he declares in "Word and Culture" (1921). And where Mayakovsky is inspired by the dregs, human and otherwise, of the modern urban streetscape, Mandelstam finds the same when he looks to the late-medieval, Parisian poet-outlaw François Villon. My own work cements all this, provisionally, with the undrying mortar of the high and low: scriptures and television, spirits and dead letters, abject sentiment and exalted wreckage. My poetry moves between introversion and energy, doubt and bravado, and between this world that is supposedly "for everyone" and the obscure ruins of a poetic history—all in an attempt to rescue what can be rescued in both.

Everything is relative and related, genitive and generative. My Haitian wife and I dragged our French-speaking Brooklyn boy to this museum of poets on the Fontanka, but he is the one who dragged me back to Russia because he wanted to meet my father. Our son is our greatest work. This book is a supplement. He already reads me like a book. This is in case he might someday grow curious about the footnotes.

—V. Vinokur

PATERNALISM

Welcome to Miami, Russian cousins,
give us your poor, your godless and vintage
Jewish woe: This is your home, you'll share
your bungalow with lizards,
coconuts and caftans. And you'll learn
English and speak it for us.

The rent is just a pinch
of cheek, and the deposit
is a gram of flesh, a zemel
flick, a moyl's wrist
is all. And you will sleep
and dream of curses that you
can't pronounce...

(if you had stayed behind with me
I'd have taught you properly
to swear round-tongued Russian oaths
my homeless son
curses fried and pickled sour-cream chilled
not like your sugary shovelfuls
of shits and fucks
like caramel in your ear)

...curses that you can't pronounce, but
curses you can hear.

THE BOOK OF IAN COURT

In the beginning was the vord,
and the vord was with bog
and the vord was bog who was
mit uns.

The same was in the beginning with bog
in the dvor, making all things, all vords,
and without him was not any thing made
that was made.

In him was life; and the life was the light of men.
And the light shine it in darkness,
and I comprehend it not.

I came just for a witness, to bear witness
of the Light, I was not that Light,
but was sent to just bear witness of that Light.
That was the true Light, in the dvor,
and the dvor was made by him,
and the dvor knew him not.

He came unto his own, and his own received him
not. This can happen sometimes,
even often.

Your image, tormenting, shifty—
My hand missed it in the fog.
"Oh my Lord!" I said mistaken,
Having meant no such thing at all.

God's name, like a massive bird,
Fled winging from my breast.
Up ahead, dense fog keeps swirling,
And behind, an empty cage
                —my hollow chest.

(1912)

from CLOUD IN PANTS

Your thought lies
dreaming on your mush of a brain
like an overfed lackey on a greasy couch,
as I rag on its bloody scrap of a heart
until I've mocked my fill, nasty and smartass.

Not one gray hair on my soul,
and no old school tenderness either.
The world shakes with the thunder of my voice,
as I go forth—a beautiful
twenty-two-year-old.

(1915)

LISTEN TO ME!

Listen to me!
If stars are lit—
doesn't that mean someone needs it?
Doesn't that mean someone wants them to be?
Doesn't that mean someone calls these spittles

                                                     pearls?

And straining
in swirls of afternoon dust,
he bursts in on God,
afraid he's too late,
weeping,
kissing His gnarled hand,
and pleads—
there should definitely be a star! —
and swears—
he won't survive this starless torture.
Then later
he wanders, worried,
but seems calm.
Says to someone:
"It's alright now, isn't it?
Not so scary?
Right?!"

Listen to me!
If stars are
lit—
doesn't that mean someone needs it?
Doesn't that make it necessary,
so that each evening
above the rooftops:
at least one star ablaze?!

(1914)

A horror high wandering flame,
How could that star be glimmering?
Transparent star, a wandering flame,
Your brother, Petroplis, is dying.

Horror high earthly dreams aflame,
A green star flying.
O, if star you are—kin to sky and water,
Your brother, Petropolis, is dying.

Monster ship on horror high
Spreading wings and flying.
Green star, in shimmering poverty
Your brother, Petropolis, is dying.

Transparent spring above the black Neva
Has broken. The wax of immortality is melting.
O, if star you are—Petropolis, your city,
Your brother, Petropolis, is dying.

(1918)

LEARNING TO LOVE

The task is learning to love
gravity, the sullen and paternal
push, keep your feet on the ground,
release the breath as the cliff
shears off into the sea that feels the rival
pull as well. The bodies of the water
find all these things acceptable, so why
can't you?

The wax, the sun, whatever, Icarus,
never mind: the goal was to fall well, to
stick the landing on the thick and
labyrinthine loam of everything that's human,
unalienable, wrong, a constellation of corrections
waiting to be made.

YOUR WORSHIP

I am your pilgrim, who wanders
to stay home; your monk,
who keeps silent when you demand
confessions and theology.

You are too difficult to love
directly; you have no roof
or floor, and I am too pious
for your rain and mud.

So I keep your shrine, the best of you,
the clean, the singing rest of you.

A stubborn priest, who knows himself
only in the dwindling oil of you,
the weeping and rebellious flame
about to die.

from ABOUT THIS

(for her and for me)

WHAT ABOUT–ABOUT THIS?

In this theme,
        so private,
            and petty,
sung through not just once
          and not thrice,
I've been spinning, a poetical squirrel,
and want to keep spinning some more.
This theme
        is now
           a Buddha prayer
and a slave knife itching for Master's neck.
And on Mars
      if there be even one human heart,
it will
      scribble and
            scrape
                at this very same thing.
This theme will come
          grab a cripple by the elbow,
drag him to a piece of paper,
           and command:
                 Go on, scribble!
And the cripple
        soars from the page
             like an eagle,
screeching bitter lines of song into the sun.
This theme will come,
          ring at the kitchen door,
Turn back,
     vanish like clover,
and then a giant
      will sprout, stand for a second,
         then crumble

and sink beneath a rippling sea of notes.
This theme will come

        and order:

                Veritas!
This theme will come

        decreeing:

                Beauty!
And even if

        you find yourself splayed on a cross,
your lips will find themselves humming a waltz.
This theme runs laps round your dizzy alphabet book—
but why bother, you thought, with something so plain!—
as it angles your

        "A"

                like sheer Mount Kazbek.
You'll get muddled,

        forget about bread, about sleep.
This theme will come,

        still fresh after decades,
just to say:

        From now on, look only at me!
And you look at her,

        and walk along with her banner,
a red silken flame flickering over the earth.
This theme is crafty!

        It dives under what happens,
ready to pounce out of secret instincts,

        —and just you try and forget her—
its fury will shake

        our souls out of their hides.
This theme turned up at my place raging,
commanding me:

        Hand over

                the reins!
Took one look at my daily cares, started making faces,
and scattered everything and everyone in a storm.
This theme came along,

        rubbing out all others,
and alone

became near and dear.
This theme put a blade to my throat.
Or like a blacksmith's hammer
                    ringing from heart to skull.
This theme darkened my day, and tells me:
Strike the dark with lines pulled from your brow.
The name
        of this
                    theme is:
        ....

I: THE BALLAD OF READING GAOL

I stood—I remember.
It gleamed.
And it was called
the Neva then.
        Mayakovsky, "Man"

The fad for ballads is not young,   About this ballad
but if the words hurt   and
and if the words say they hurt,   about any ballads
then even the ballad fad grows young.
Lubyansky Drive.
        Vodopyany Lane.
                            Set
and
                            Scene.
She.
                    Lying in bed.
He.
        Telephone on the table.
"He" and "She", that's my ballad.
Not terribly new.
What's terrible is
        "He" is "Me"
and "She"
            has to do with me.

Why jail?
       It's Christmas.
                All bustles.
No bars on these windows.
But never mind that.
           Like I said—jail.
The table.
       On the table, a reed.

I touch it, barely—and blisters flare.   A number
The horn flies from my hands.   released
Out of the trademark stamp   through the cable
two bright arrows
shoot telephone lightning.
And next door.
       From one room over,
              drowsy:
"When, what?
           Where's the stuck pig?"
The ringer already squealing from burns,
the phone molten-white.
She's sick!
      In bed!
Run!
      Quick!
         It's time!
My flesh is smoking, a smothered searing.
Lightning running up and down my body.
Pressed and clutched by a million volts.
My lip bumps into the telephone furnace.
And through the drill holes
            of the house,
Ploughing up
           Myasnitsky St.,
ripping apart
         the cable,
the number
         flies like bullet
    to the switchboard girl.

Her eyes are drowsy—
holidays you work double.
Another red light.
She's calling!
          The lamp goes out.
And all the sudden
          a blinking impish play,
the whole network shreds.
—67-10!
Connect me!
          Vodopyany Lane!
                              Quick!

Oh boy!
Or else the electricity builds up—
and on the night before Christmas
          you'll be blown sky high
along with
          your whole
                    telephone station.
Once upon a time there was an old man who lived
on Myasnitskaya for a hundred years —
and for that hundred years
          he would tell
                    his grandchildren
about this.
—It was—a Saturday...
                    before a Sunday...
Out for a bit of ham...
          Wanted to buy it cheap...
Then someone, somewhere, somehow: crack!..
                    An earthquake...
My feet are hot...
          boot-soles shake!.. —
The kids don't buy it,
          the who
                    and the where
                              and the how of it.
An earthquake?
          In winter?
                    At the Central Post Office?!

Squeezing a miracle through its shoelace-thin   The telephone
                                    cord,   pounces
the ear horn stretches, gaping,   on all
a ringing thunder smothers the silence,
a belch of lava beneath the telephone jangle.
This shrill
          ringing drill
scorched its way into the walls
                    trying to blow up what's left.
Pealing echoes,
          thousands of them,
                    ricochet
                              off the walls,
rolling under the chairs,
                    under the bed.
The abominable bell leaps from the ceiling
and smacks the floor.
And then again,
          like a slap-happy basketball
bounces against the ceiling from the floor,
and a ringing rain of splinters falls.
Every window pane
          and every fireplace damper
were moved to harmonize in telephone tone.
Shaking
          the house
                    like a rattle,
a telephone drowning in its own ringing flood.

Sleep swollen   Call for a second
          pinpoint eyes
prickling through fired cheeks.
The cook gets up, sluggish,
walks over,
          grunting and groaning.
Her head like a stewed apple.
Her brow wrinkled by thinking.
—Who?
          Vladim Vladimych?!
                    Oh! —

Waddles off, slippers flapping.
Walks.
          Measuring paces, like a proper second.
Her footsteps recede...
              Hardly hear them...
And the rest of the world steps aside
as the unknown takes aim at me
down the barrel of a telephone.

Conference panelists of the world   Enlightening
freeze in mid-gesture.   the world
Just like that,
          mouths gaping
                in my direction
at the Christmas to end all Christmas.
Seems like they live
                squabble to squabble.
Their home
                a daily blah.
They look at me
                    like a mirror,
and wait for the single combat of my deadly love.
The howling sirens turn to stone.
The spinning wheels and footsteps cease.
Just the clearing for the duel,
          and doctor-time standing by
with the endless bandage of all-healing death.

(1923)

RE:

To all the titular councilors I've loved:
I, too, have listened to the wisdom of
Pomeranians and Lhasa apsos, taking care
to ignore the empty kvetching of toy poodles.

At this time I can confirm that there is a devil
behind every medal, and that a court chamberlain
doesn't have an eye in the middle of his forehead,
at least not the court chamberlain I examined.

The departmental director, however, is not a cork,
He really is a director. He flatly refuses to float.
And the strange things happening in Spain
are simply the strange things that happen in Spain.

Let the Spaniards worry.

WESTCLOX

In times like these
I keep an old pocket watch
Against my heart.
It tells her not to skip
Or run, lest she
Stumble and break.

And medical opinions
Swarm in squabbles
Over its radiating
Radium dials—
Those hands so calm
That glow across
The ring of glowing
Numbers, lines,
Those happy, steady beacons
That work to make
A steady tumor
Of my heart.

BECAUSE THEODICY

Because she was old and tired and her heart
        stopped beating
Because the surface of the earth is a bunch of plates
        that rub against each other
Because he was a bad guy and was jealous of the Jews
Because bad guys are people too
Because it was an accident
Because we have laws and policemen
Because sometimes I get angry just like you do
Because that's what happens when you fly big airplanes
        into tall buildings
Because your uncle and cousins were at home
        when the earthquake came
Because he gave in to his anger, slaughtered
        the Sand People, and betrayed the Jedi
Because the Clones were trained to follow orders
        no matter what
Because there was no food left in Leningrad
Because it's expensive to live in New York
Because at first the Germans and the Russians
        were on the same team
Because that idiot almost ran us over
Because a German bomb exploded and a piece of it
        went through his lung
Because I would have gone to jail if I had
Because nobody caught him
Because jail was too good for him
Because he wanted to, probably just because
        he realized that he could
Because what if my enemies don't deserve to die
Because if you live long enough you will have enemies
Because I was there
Because sometimes it feels like he exists and sometimes
        like he doesn't
Because I wasn't talking to you
Because I'm not God
Because I didn't know what to tell you

Because it looked like a huge cigar crumbling
        under the weight of its ash
Because of gravity
Because without gravity we'd float up into space
        like the silver balloons
Because I wanted to throw up but didn't
        know why I couldn't
Because that won't happen for three billion years
Because usually that doesn't happen
Because I promise that won't happen to us
Because these things happen for a reason
Because all kinds of things can happen anytime
        for no good reason
Because I'm old and tired and want to go back to sleep

ARIADNE

       & she weaves the thread
as she pulls deeper
          into the heart of the
heart of the labyrinth
      drawn by the echoes
the scent of open flesh
          mysterious and familiar
writing on the walls
      hieroglyphs in fingernail
and blood pulling her
          closer to the horns the
fur the sad and moist
      black eyes of a dilemma

for what relative is closer
          than the minotaur our
brother our marrow our
      meat and our fat our
death and deliverance our
          guide deliberating over
fate as if fate was the
      way to lay hands on
the soul of the soul

but no one knows better
          than the son of pasiphae
that nothing can be known
      inside these corridors
the nothing that is known
          in the layer after layer
of the onion that is sweet
      and makes you cry

daedalus had to make
      two labyrinths
a dance underground
a pirouette in the air

and all he wanted of life
was to live on the surface
a wife a son a jug of wine
cheap and happy and rich
as the loam caressed between
      the sun and the earth
            and the sea

Sleeplessness. Omeros. Taut sails.
I have read the list of ships halfway:
This lengthened brood, this train of cranes,
That once took off from Hellas.

Like a wedge of cranes towards strangers' shores—
On the heads of kings there foams a holy frenzy—
Where are you sailing to? Were it not for Helen,
What is Troy alone to you, Achaian husbands?

And the sea and Homer—all things are moved by love.
Who then should I listen to? And now Homer is silent,
While the black sea, oratund, roars soft
And with weighty thunder laps gently at my bed.

(1915)

THE DEADLIEST CATCH

Sparrows tucked into his tunic, two
sword hilts and a whetstone carved
like the head of a bull, a pine cone
dipped in nectar or blood, knees
forearms calf muscles rippling across
three thousand years: Ashurnasirpal
tending to the Tree of Life, his beard
like a carpet of
beads

Sing in me, Muse, of the wickedness
of tuna and the majesty of
crab upon the wine-dark sea

Ninevah and Nimrud, Ishtar and
Ishtar, Isis and ISIS and ISIL, a love
greater than any understanding,
but smaller than any love I have
understood, takes the captives by the
hair, an incision at the thyrohyoid
ligament, streaming banners, Apanasenko
radiant, stick the nurses, stick
the Poles, Thestor son of Enops
in his fine polished chariot trembling as
Patroclos hooks the mouth and pulls
him over the rail like a
Northern Bluefin, blinding
bright scales washed
dark in the wine red red
stuff

Let the Earth Clean Your Teeth
in the morning, let the earth
clean your teeth at the end
of the day, let the earth clean
my teeth in the grave

VERSES ON AN UNKNOWN SOLDIER

I
Let this air be called as a witness—
With its long-range, high-caliber heart—
While in the trenches, omnivorous, busy,
There's an ocean, a windowless stuff.

How these stars can be nosy:
Always they stare, and for what?
In judgment of judge and of witness,
In an ocean, a windowless stuff.

Rain remembers, a taciturn sower,
In that anonymous manna of his,
A thick forested ocean of crosses
Marking a regimental wedge.

There'll be people, frozen and puny,
There to kill and to freeze and to starve,
And beneath his illustrious headstone
Is where the unknown soldier will rest.

Teach me, you puny swallow,
Yourself having unlearned to fly,
How might I from this aerial sepulcher
So wingless and rudderless try?

And for Lermontov, for Mikhail's sake,
I will hand you the strictest account,
How a sepulcher tutors the hunchback,
How a pit in the air can attract.

II
Like grape bunches shivering, slithering,
These fat planets imperil us all,
Like cities stolen and dangling,
Gold-plated slips of tongue, tattletales,
Cold poison berries, expanding
tents, gold constellations, fat of the stars.

III
Through ether denoted decimally,
Light ground to a fine ray of speeds,
Comes a digit made clear and diaphanous:
Light zeroes, bright pain, white moths.

Past the field of all fields is a new field
Gliding crane-like, triangularly—
The news glides down a dusting of light—
It's still bright after yesterday's fray.

The news glides down a dusting of light:
I'm not Leipzig, not Waterloo, not
The Battle of Nations, I'm—something new—
At my birth light's way will be lit.

In the depths of the black-marble oyster
The flicker of Austerlitz dies—
A mediterranean swallow will flinch,
And the plague sands of Egypt will churn.

IV
The Arabian mince meal, a mishmash,
Light ground to a fine ray of speeds,
And with his crooked soles slanted and planted
On my retina, a well-balanced ray.

Millions dead, killed inexpensively,
Stamped a visible trail in the void—
Pleasant dreams and best wishes to all of them,
On behalf of these underground forts.

Incorruptible heaven of trenches,
A heaven of wholesale trench death,
After you—and from you—(you buy everyone)—
I rush off, lips first, in the dark.

Past the craters, the bulwarks and mudslides,
All the places he lingered and dimmed,
Goes the overturned, overcast, pockmarked,
The groveling Genius of graves.

V

Ground troops know how to die well,
Just as night choirs know how to sing well
Of Schweik's flattened grin
And of Quixote's songbird spear
And of the knight's iron claw.
And the cripple makes friends with the conscript:
There's work for them both to be found.
Wooden clatter, a brood of crutches
Skirting the edge of our Age: Workers
Of the world, comrades, onward! Inherit the earth!

VI

Is that why the skull must develop,
Fill the brow, temple to temple,
So that a downpour of regiments couldn't
But fill its sockets—so precious, so dear?
From life the skull will develop,
Fill the brow, temple to temple,
Teasing itself, in stitches seamless and pure,
Comprehension will brighten its cupola,
Foaming with thought, a dream of itself—
Cup of cups, a father of fatherlands—
A stitch of stars lines your bonnet—
Shakespeare's father, most happy cap.

VII

Sycamore keen, poplar sheen,
A bit blushing, straight home they will go,
As if swooning, so faintly flickering,
They charm heaven above and below.
For us only excess is brotherly,
And ahead: no abyss, just a hole,
And to battle for air that is habitable
Is a glory without any peer.

So that's why the tare was made ready,
Made so pretty out there in the void,
So the pale stars, a bit blushing,
Could run straight back, all the way home.

With my consciousness charmed
By half-conscious existence,
I've no choice but to sup of this cookery
And eat my own head under fire.

Night, stepmother of this horde of stars,
What will it be—now and then after?

VIII
Our aortas fill up with blood,
Down the columns, a whispering sound:
I was born 'ninety-four,
I was born 'ninety-two...
And through the herd and the crowd, my fist
Clenching the tattered year of my birth,
My lips all but bloodless, I whisper:
I was born on the night midst the second
And third of January, in 'ninety-one,
Unreliable year, and the centuries—
A ring of fire, my hedge of flame.

(1937)

TRY THIS ONE WEIRD ISAIAH

In my Feed, the wolf dwells with the lamb,
and the leopard lies down with the kid; and
the calf and the young lion and the fatling together;
and a little child sleeps with his puppy through
time-lapse photomontage.

In my Feed, the wolf and the lamb shall feed
together, and the lion shall eat straw
like the bullock: and dust shall be
the serpent's meat, and serpent's meat
shall be the new millennial dinner hack,
and no more shall there be takeout on
Prospect Mountain.

Dads will finish their Bachelor's Degrees and
meet Christian Singles, the Crystal
Palace shall be affordably 3D
printed, and you won't believe

what happens next.

LET'S MAKE A DEAL

Waiting was the favorite game show

       if mother wasn't home before 8
I would hold the knife in my teeth, lurking
in the thickening shadows of our efficiency
apartment, like a tiny Martin Sheen stripped
down to Marlow.

You're not worried something happened
to your mother, she'd laugh, you're afraid they'd
come for you after they were done with me.

Nobody loses at the waiting game—

Door Number 1: The End!
Door Number 2: More Waiting!

SURVIVORMAN

If you are thirsty drink
your piss, maybe—

This is how the human race survives

—but never seawater

If you sweat on a cold day
take off your clothes and dry
yourself with snow

Nearly everything is a good source
of protein, which will

make you thirsty. So

Stay sharp and

avoid sharp rocks

always keep moving

downstream uphill

to orient yourself

rest is the most important

and shelter

when confronted with a wild

animal keep moving keep

the camera rolling

hold your ground and

run.

NAKED & AFRAID

John Milton should get a writing credit
for blurring out the no-longer-private
parts of these hardy Adams and Eves, their
fat melting, ague wracked, skin beset by
plagues unknown to Eden: *Dam. Tzefardea.*
Kinim. Arov. Blood. Frogs. Lice. Beasts.
Pestilence. Boils. Hail. Locusts. Darkness.
The Death of Unearned Dignity.

Better to rule in Hell than be naked and
afraid in Heaven.

After 21 days with Amber and Trent, we
have re-experienced the Fortunate Fall
into food and fabric and facebook, and
yet their Primitive Survival Rating
has increased by a measly 1.2.

The jeep drives through the extraction
point almost without stopping, the brown
driver doing his best not to stare at the
two white sacks of flayed skin exulting—
totally stoked—sacrifices

                        to Xipe Totec,
god of goldsmiths
                        and abundance.

HANNIBALISM

I know why I watch

on the screen serial
killers are not about
the murder it's all
about becoming

moths born to the flame
and always William Blake
Lambs and Tygers Great
Red Dragons chrysalises great
watersheds of skin a great
big fat person puts the lotion
in the basket

I know why I watch

all these desperate
transformations trans-
substantiations gods
knowing mortals becoming
gods becoming mortals

then again maybe it is
about the murder a little bit

I know why I watch

I watch myself unchanging watch

and there I am there I

am there

THE SHARK TANK

Their shark eyes don't blink until the sharks
are ready for the kill, their shark teeth
laughing as the sharks call each other
vampires and termites and leeches and
parasites.

Sitting in the kitchen, I think I
really bring a lot to the table, 43 years:

- or 43 as of tomorrow
- drawing breath 24/7/365
- consistent multiple revenue
- streams through my veins cash
- flows through my lymphatic vessels

- and a 15% stake at $200,000 is a
- more than fair valuation of my equity
- at half-life

But What Do The Sharks Think?

Shark 1: Even if you deserve another 43, will you be
the sort of 86-year-old who will be missed?
I admire the enthusiasm, but I have to say
I'm out.

Shark 2: Every birthday, there you are doing
your goddamn taxes. I just don't understand
the product and you don't have a
business, so I'm out.

Shark 3: I don't trust you for a second, so I will
offer you $100 for 51%, but I will let you
keep your family (minus expenses and
ageing parents), 75% of the
teeth in your face and 60% of the
hair on your head.

Fuck this, I tell myself, I was holding out for Mark Cuban,
slouching in his eternal chair: a High Priest of Indifference.

PROTOCOLS OF THE REAL LEARNED HOUSEWIVES OF AUSCHWITZ-BIRKENSTOCKS

Rudolf Höss was the housewife who
said: I'm not here to make friends.

Afterwards, Adorno of the Magi spake: after
Auschwitz, poetry is impossible
and all that is left are heaps
of possibly poetry, piles of anapests,
trucks of trochees, iambs
of prosthetic limbs.

You see the problem. Design.
You see the solution. Disrupt.

It's like what that guy Himmler said:
In my world, money doesn't talk.
It swears.

We live, no, I live, no, you,
no, no, but yes, something lives
without feeling
the earth underfoot, a dream of
a seventy-year-dead figure-

of-speech, dwells barbarically
auf dieser Erde, underfoot there is
only poetry, sharp like smashed
Paschal plates, the crumbs
of the winged bulls of Ninevah.

TWO PACKS A DAY

I've been considering giving up
biblical references altogether. I mean,

When I say Genesis, do you think of Jacob
and Esau, or Peter Gabriel versus Phil Collins?

When I say Egypt, do you think of Potiphar
and Joseph, or Sadat and the Muslim Brotherhood?

When I say Isaiah, do you think Prophets
or Pistons? And Amos, why is he so Famous?

When I say "that's just an antediluvian, pre-
lapsarian jeremiad," are you insulted?

And what am I thinking when I say
Genesis? What am I thinking when I say
Exodus? I know what I'm thinking
when I say Leviticus, but that's just
because I'm a dirty old man, and it's
none of your business.

Everyone is entitled to one vice
in their old age (Proverbs 32).

STORAGE WARS

The Soul
/just kidding/
—Vsevelod Nekrasov

And now I should wish to describe to you briefly
what is in my soul.

Across the street, a hospital was torn down in my soul
to make way for luxury condominiums, its façade left
standing out of respect or something.

In my soul, there is an unattractive man sitting
in his warm half-basement, worried about wet snow.

An old lady in my soul is spitting tfu tfu tfu
kinehora but we both know what's the difference.

In my soul all went as I wished
and all went badly.

The other day I told my soul I would prefer not to.
My soul was not amused.

Stop hoarding! I told my soul.
My soul was embarrassed and prideful.

My soul gets first-category rations
and would like to share them
with every other soul: Here, soul, eat!
But I remind my soul
that there are shortages.

In my soul, I thought, Why do I always
have to be the bad guy.
When the inside of my soul
is auctioned off on A&E, I would like
the bidding to start at $150.

I am convinced there are rare coins
in my soul that only the right buyer
will find and appreciate.

My soul replies Yeah keep telling that
to yourself buddy.

/Well that's fine I will, I will keep
telling that to myself because after all
        what else
        if not that
        is the infamous
        immortality
        of the soul./

TRISTIA

I've learned the science of parting,
Of bare heads, plaintive outbursts in the night.
The oxen chew, anticipation lengthens
On this last vigil of the city watch.
And I honor the rites of this cock-crowing night,
When I take up my stick and satchel of sorrows,
And look far to the distance with weeping eyes,
When women weeping sound like Muses singing.

Who can tell from the word "parting"
What sort of separation is in store for us?
What does the rooster promise in his outburst,
While the fire still burns on the acropolis,
On the dawn of a new life of some sort,
While the lazy oxen chew their cud,
Why does the rooster, herald of new life,
Beat his wings upon the city walls?

And I do love the way yarn works:
The shuttle flickers and the spindle hums.
And look there, she's floating towards us
Like swan's down, barefoot Delia!
O' thin root of our life,
How poor the language of rejoicing!
All of this took place before, all will repeat,
And yet the moment of recognition is so sweet.

Let it be so: a clear shape forms
On the clean clay dish,
Stretched like a squirrel pelt,
The girl bends down to see the wax.
Not for us to guess on Greek Erebus,
Wax is to women what bronze is to men.
Our fate comes to us in battles,
Death comes to them in divination.

(1918)

THE TRISTIA OF COUNT SHEREMETIEV II

for Faina and Luba

The flight left at six in the morning,
and we had to be there eight hours
ahead of time. In the lobby we sat
around the mound of luggage: pallid
boxes, flat-chested suitcases growing
colder as the hour approached.

The conveyor belt begins.
My grandmother—rubles and amber
hiding in the lining of her coat,
nervous, as the old officer vents:
"All right yidels, give up the diamonds!

"Mind yourselves, I used to be nasty,
shipped plenty off to Solovki in my day!"
But he softens when he figures out
my mother was without her husband:
"You're not forsaking us,
you're running from your man."
He moves us through, and the conveyor ends.

Across the glass barrier our relatives drown
in the dim algae of Moscow's international airport,
waving feebly, pleading (write write write).
and suddenly our tongues ache
like clappers in the muffled bells
of our Russian mouths: Goodbye life,
bye bye death (write write write)...

PROCESS THEOLOGY

Father who art in heaven
hallowed be, be hollowed
as my father who art on earth.
Father who art, father who aren't,
lead me not into the hollow,
into the daily donut, into privation.

Forgive my debts, forgive my debtors,
forget my bets, ignore my betters.
And lead me not, and lead me not,
and let me not, and let me never
be in tentation, but waive delivery,
for shipping is evil and thine
is the kingdom and is it ever.

PIGEON MILK

In my father's house, my head hits the lamp
in my half-sister's room, which was my room
until I was six. Long-haired cats rub against me

unaffectionately, shedding disapproval
on my strange clothes and foreign skin.

My father measures how far my head reaches over his
thickly salted crown: "Nu, *amerikanetz*, isn't it true
we want our descendants to be better off,
or maybe just better than we were?"

I have outgrown my bones, but I can fit
my entire collection of emotions (six of them)
into this old room with her fold-out sofa and icons,
cat books and encyclopedias, photographs
of a moody 12-year-old girl who is half me
but whom I have not yet met.

Through the thin Brezhnev walls, the black smell
of the frying pan, a dull sizzle of television, the waters
part and drown all of the delights of Egypt—
dollar fleshpots, golden chains and chariots.

And like a prodigal patriarch, Father asks:
"What the devil have you been doing
              over there?"

MAMAN DLO

The ocean is a good place to hide things.

I would bare my thin ribs to the dull-then-
stinging fists of surf, saying "I can take you,
can't knock me down." Nobody heard me,
and the water kept things between friends.

My mother claimed the ocean saved her
daily, as she blew her nose below the surface
and called me away from the stubborn sand
to join her and hide in its warm cheek.

The ocean is a good place to hide things,
you can stash a lucky sugar cube there forever.
And when you dip a brush or a reed
into its green dark, the water won't laugh,
it will perfectly understand.

SILENTIUM

She has not yet been born,
She is both word and music,
And by this, the unbreakable
Bond between everything that lives.

The bosom of the sea breathes calmly,
But the day gleams like a lunatic,
While pale lilac foams
In its blackened azure bowl.

May my own lips attain
This most primeval muteness,
Like a crystalline note,
Immaculate since birth.

Remain as foam, o' Aphrodite,
And word, return to music,
And heart, by heart be chastened,
Poured out from fundamental life.

(1910, 1935)

No need to discuss anything,
There's nothing to be learned:
How melancholy and how goodly
Is the animal's dark soul.

It wants to teach you nothing,
It cannot speak at all
And swims off, a young dolphin
On the gray gulfs of the world.

(1909)

Oh, how we love to play the hypocrite
And then forget so easily
How we are more close to death in childhood
Than in our riper years.

The cranky child still tugs
His grievance from his dish,
But I've got no one to pout at
And I'm alone on every path.

But I don't want to slumber like a fish
In the watery coma of the deep,
And I have a free choice of roads
Among my sufferings and cares.

[The beast molts, the fish plays
In the watery coma of the deep—
And if only one didn't have to look at the twists
Of people's sufferings, people's cares.]*

(1932)

*Mandelstam's earlier version of the last stanza

GETTING ALONG WITH HORSES

Hooves struck.
Like song:
—Clip.
Clop.
Clep.
Clup.—

The wind stripped
street, an ice
shod slide.
A horse crashed
on its rump, and
right away
one slack-jaw after another
came down Kuznetsky
in bell-bottoms to have a look-

                         see,

crowding round,
a jingle jangle of laughter:
—Horse fell! —
—Fallen horse! —
All Kuznetsky Street laughed,
Except for me,
I didn't mix my voice into that howl.
I walk up
and I see
the horse eyes...

The street toppled over,
flowing how it likes...
I walk up and I see
drop from drop
rolling down its face,
burrowing in its hide...

And some kind of common
animal anguish

splashed and poured out of me
and dissolved in a rustle.
"Horse, please, don't.
Listen to me, horse—
do you think you're any less than they are?
Little one,
all of us are horses, sort of,
every one of us a horse in his own way."
Maybe the old nag
didn't need a nanny,
maybe she thought my notion seemed a little

                            stale,

but
the horse
gave a jerk,
stood on its legs,
neighed
and off she went.
Flicking its tail.
Chestnut, childlike.
Came home cheerful,
stood in its stall.
And the whole time she felt
like a colt,
and life was worth living,
and work worthwhile.

(1918)

A JAKE'S JACKET

I will sew myself black trousers
from the velvet of my voice.
A yellow jacket out of three lengths of sunset.
Down the Nevsky *monde*, down its polished latitudes,
I'll step along like Don Juan in profile.

Let the earth cry out, all sissy soft from slumber:
"You're off to have your way with spring!"
As for the sun, I'll offer an obnoxious grin and say:
"Look how the pavement rolls me along like a French r!"

And isn't it because the sky is blue,
and the earth is my lover girl in birthday clothes,
that I can give you poems, jolly ones, like be-bi-bo,
and sharp and needful ones, like toothpicks!

Ladies, lovers of my prime cuts,
and that one girl who's looking at me
like I was her brother,
bury me in tossed smiles—
I'll sew your garlands into a jake's jacket!

(1914)

WHO'S YOURS

If Derrida was my Daddy I would have been raised
by Lionel Jospin, which would have made it difficult
to maintain my avowedly apolitical stance.

I'm rolling in the playground sand again,
strange men attending to my mother.
If she's Queen Gertrude, why is Hamlet
so eager to make King H a ghost?

I detest the expression, but there it is.
Can that dude be my Daddy?
That was a request. That was a question.
That was my answer. Good sir,
my answer stands.

HAVING YOURS

In my dream my wife and my mother are laughing.
An army surgeon opens Grandpa Iliusha's ribbed back
like a hinged shutter and puts back the lung
he had cut out—there had been no shrapnel in it after all.
My grandmother eats leisurely, as the Germans encircle
Leningrad with a string of bratwurst.

My junior high biology teacher takes out a slide
of Grandpa Lyonia's cancerous lungs—
a thin slice of dirty sponge—
and replaces it with firm pinkness.
In my dream I am plump and jolly.
In my dream there are no dreams,

Just as there is no need for hope.
In my dream I go outside to watch eleven sons
take deep breaths and see who can stay
underwater the longest and blow out
eleven birthday cakes with eleven candles
in one firm pink puff.

A MECHANISM FOR BLOOD

My mother's father fixed watches, clocks.
Evenings he'd be moonlighting,
little hammers hitting little picks and gears,
tick-tick.

His heart struggled to make up
for the lung he lost on the Byelorussian Front,
where a tipsy field surgeon had to saw
through his back and break into the case
of his ribs.

He watched me until I was eight months old
and his heart would go no further, pulling
my carriage, tinkling with formula empties
and vodka bottles, through Napoleon's mud,
my eyes shaking for the branches naked above.

At home, he would put me on his chest,
gather my fingers into fists, and say,
"Beat Grandpa, *molodets,*
tock-tock!"

THE SPECIALIST

Doctor, call Ivan the Terrible, quick.

Pull out these eyes: I don't need
to see anything more or less beautiful.
Why does everyone assume the architect
of St. Basil's Cathedral mourned his sight?

Peel back my skin: it has little
to caress and little to protect.

Fold my ears into their canals:
these leaky boats are fit
for mothballs and museums.

Replace my nose with a silver hump:
it has no place to lodge (and I probably
have some sort of social disease anyway).

My palate is my nose's cousin, so
they must be collaborators. Hot lead will do.

And last: my tongue. Take only some of it,
just the part that wanders or
forgets. Leave a stump for vowels
so that I may be recognized, like Moses
stammering before the angry crowds.

from OCTAVES

Tell me, draftsman of the desert,
Geometer of Arab sands,
Could the unruliness of lines
Be stronger than the blowing wind?
—Doesn't concern me, all the fuss
of his Judaic cares—
He forms forms from formlessness
And drinks formlessness from forms...

(1934)

Deaf words...
Judea turned to stone,
And his head drooped
Heavier with every passing beat.

Soldiers stood around,
Kept watch over the waning body;
The halo head hung like a twig
On someone else's slender stem.

And He ruled and drooped
Like a lily in its native slough,
And the depths, where reed-stems drown,
Gloried in its law.

(1910)

ABRAM MEETS THE MAKER

(after Bereshit Rabbah 39:2 and Midrash Ha-Gadol Gen 12:1)

Is this castle without a master?
He never leaves, there is no door,
does his own laundry, rags
gleaming wet across the slate
black roof. Is this the castle
you were looking for?

Is this the castle without a master?
Rags gleaming from wires
banners aflame, stout columns
of flame holding down the black
slate roof. Call a fire brigade,
no door to break down. Is this
the castle we were looking for?

Is this that castle without the master,
the laundering, fire-breathing
hermit, that master, washing
his garment by morning,
burning his garment by night,
and hidden by battlements, always
spinning, weaving, always?

THE BOOK OF GENESIS

On the eighth day, the Discus Fish
was gone. His life was brief, but
one can get attached in minutes.

The aquarium was hopeless now.
We still fed the others—Black Mollies,
Gourami Sunbursts, Congo Tetras;
even added other tenants, Fancy Guppies,
Leopard Catfish, but stopped
caring when we had to go away and
dropped dissolvable vacation feeders
in the sweaty water.

After the Discus died, we accepted
quarrels, losses, small aquarium disasters,

and each no longer seemed a complication,
but only one more sad relief, referring to the last.

LENINGRAD

I've come back to my city, familiar to tears,
To life's little veins and puffed childhood glands.

You've come back. . . Quick, open and swallow
Your fish oil from the river lamps of Leningrad.

Quick now, think of that Decembery day,
The nasty tar with a bit of yolk whipped in.

Oh Petersburg, I don't want to die just yet:
You still have my phone numbers.

Petersburg, I still have the addresses—
They could lead me to the voices of the dead.

I live on the back stair, and the bell,
Ripped out flesh and all, keeps beating in my head.

And so I wait through the night for my guests to arrive,
Rattling these door chains, these convict shackles.

(1930)

OF THE FATHER TONGUE

Never tempt a native language.
Its roots are thin and deep.

Just when you think the old words
have forgotten you, then
the summer poplars burst and you
are tarred and feathered in a snow
of slurry endings.

Genitive, genitive, who owns whom?
This is late June in Petersburg,
there is no night to hide in here.

In any case you live under the name of the father,
like an eel darting from its rock at curious hands.

And now you've come back,
quick, open wide while the potato
words are hot. Repeat after me:

Preposition accepted, I take it all back,
Petersburg, I don't want to be born
just yet.

The golden ray of honey poured out of the bottle
So thick and slow, that the lady of the house had time enough
                                        to murmur:
—Here, in sad Tauris, where we have been deposited
                                        by fate,
We are never bored, —she said and glanced over her shoulder.

The rites of Bacchus everywhere, as though the world were only
Guards and hounds, —you walk around and see no one.
The days peacefully roll by, like heavy barrels.
Far-away voices in a hut—you cannot understand, you cannot
                                        respond.

After tea we went out into the great brown garden,
Dark curtains drawn over the windows, like eyelashes.
We walked past white columns to see the vineyard,
Its sleepy hills wet with the glassy air.

I said: Grapevines thrive in this antique battle,
Wild-haired horsemen charging the hills in curly rows.
The science of Hellas among the stones of Tauris,
Highborn golden acres rusting in these furrows.

While in the white room silence spins its wheel,
Smelling of vinegar, paint, wine fresh from the cellar.
Do you remember, at home in Greece, a wife beloved by all—
Not Helen, but the other one—how long she kept on weaving?

Golden fleece, where are you then, golden fleece?
His whole way serenaded by the crash of waves,
Scuttling his ship and its sea-bruised sails,
Odysseus returned, full with time and space.

(1917)

WHO DOES

For Neil Gordon

"It's too bad she won't live. But then again, who does?"
–Hampton Fancher

When do we get to live
When does the scaffolding come down
When will the blood be refreshed
the marrow restored or replaced
like changing the oil once and for all
When will the broken bones
grow back stronger—the cancellous
and the cortical weaving
into a mineral matrix
brighter than before

When does the party start
I'm holding my breath
I've been holding my breath
I won't hold my breath much longer
Let's get this party started—quickly
and don't you dare start
without me

When will I see by faith
that beautiful land
or see by unfaith
that ambrosial fruit
of life's tree—fair
or unfair

I'm no sucker
though could be I'm the first
and the last sucker on earth
spinning like a beach ball
of death at the center—a nest
of wasps sucking
on the planet's axis

The golden nectar pours
so slowly—
there's time
enough to say
every viscous thing
there ever was
to say

Armed with the eyes of slender wasps,
Sucking at the planet's axis, planet's axis,
I can feel all there ever was to witness,
And recall it by heart though it's pointless.

But I do not draw and do not sing,
And I don't drag black hairs across a string:
I only take great gulps of life and love
To envy the most clever and almighty wasps.

O, if only some day—evading sleep and
Death—the summer heat and stinging air
Could prick my ear to hear the spinning
Of the planet's axis, planet's axis.

(1937)

LETTER FROM PARIS TO COMRADE KOSTROV ABOUT THE ESSENCE OF LOVE

Please forgive
                me,
                                Comrade Kostrov,
with your characteristic
                        breadth of soul,
for blowing
                part of the lines
you allotted to Paris
                        on lyrics.
Just imagine:
                a beauty
                                enters,
wrapped
        in beads and furs.
I
  took this beauty
                and I said:
—did I say right
                or wrong now?—
I come from Russia,
                        Comrade,
well-known in my land am I,
I've seen
        girls more beautiful
I've seen
        girls with better figures.
And girls
                prefer poets.
Cause I'm clever
                and full-throated,
I can talk your teeth off—
if only
        you agree to listen.

Can't snare
                me
                        with crap,

with a passing
                pair of whims.
Love
        has wounded me
                        for good—
can barely drag myself about.
I can't
        measure love
                    with weddings:
She's unloved me—
                    sailed away.
I mean it,
        Comrade,
I couldn't give a spit
                    for cupolas.
So now we're getting into details,
right, enough jokes,
my beauty,
            I'm not twenty, —
rather, thirty...
                and then some.
Love
    lies not
            in harder boiling,
lies not
        in burning coals,
it lies
        in that which rises beyond hills of breasts
over
    hair-jungles.

To love—
        means this:
                        to run
deep into the yard
                with a gleaming axe,
chop wood
                until the rook-black night,
flaunting all
            your
                strength.

To love—
        is to tear yourself
                away from sheets torn
by insomnia,
        jealous of Copernicus,
because he,
        and not some Jane Doe husband
is
        my
                rival.
Love
        for us
                is no bushy paradise,
Love
        for us
                is a humming that tells us
that the stalled motor
        of the heart
                just got started up again.
You
        broke the thread
                to Moscow.
Years—
        distance.
Just how
        could I
                explain
this situation to you?
Skyful of lights
                upon the earth...
Hellful of stars
                upon the deep blue sky.
If I were
        not a poet,
I would be
        an astrologer.
The square begins to buzz,
traffic spins,
I walk around,
                scribbling poems
                    in a little notebook.

Cars
      zip
            along
without knocking me down.
The clever fellows
            get it:
here is a man—
            in ecstasy.
A crowd of sights
            and insights
brimming
      to the lid.
Here
      even bears
might grow wings.
And so
      out of some
            greasy cafeteria,
once all this
      comes to a boil,
from gut
      to star
            the word yawns
like a golden-born comet.
The tail
      splashed
            across a third of the sky,
its plumage
      burns and sparks,
so that two lovers
            could admire the stars
from their
      lilac arbor.
So that weak eyes
      could be lifted,
            led,
                  and lured.
So that hostile
      heads
            could be sawed from shoulders

by this long-tailed
    glittering sword.
As for myself—
   until the last thump inside my chest,
I will linger,
   as though I'm on a date—
I overhear myself:
   love will ever start and hum—
so simple,
   human.
Hurricane,
   fire,
     water
rumble forward.
Who
   could
     control this?
Can you?
   Go ahead, try...

(1929)

NOTRE DAME

Where Roman justice judged another race
Stands a basilica, exuberant and primal,
Like Adam once before, its nerves splash forth,
Its muscles play inside the airy, cross-shaped dome.

But from outside, a secret plan appears:
Here the flying buttresses took care
So that the heavy mass can't crush the walls,
So the cupolic battering ram is still.

Metrical labyrinth, forest unfathomable,
The Gothic soul—its rational abyss,
Egyptian might, Christian timidity,
An oak beside a reed, and the plumb is czar throughout.

But the more carefully, oh citadel of Notre Dame,
I learned your monstrous ribs,
The more and more I thought: from unkind heaviness
Someday I too might create loveliness.

(1912)

CONCERT AT ST. PAUL'S CHAPEL
FULTON STREET, JULY 2001

All of the city's American flags
have bivouacked in Lower Manhattan.

Outside: the symphony of concrete,
taxicabs, the tap shoes of high finance.

While inside St. Paul's Chapel—
restored into a marshmallow of pink
and white and baby blue—our bodies
are suffused with Schubert, Hindemith,
Beethoven. And the culture speculators
move slow, like convalescents, their mouths
agape from music or from before.

Health dictates I must unlearn the pleasures
of the pleasant, the useless plucking
of the holy and sublime, the choking fumes
of empathy, the chords of kindness.
Better to resound with the plain
acoustics of existence, the thud of bread
and peace and shiny shoes.

FROM THE OTHER END

Everyone is writing garden poems
and I want a garden poem of my own,
but all my arugula can think of is
sex—an orgy of little yellow flowers
for me to prune like a parent screening
phone calls.

My pot of herbs resides at the edge
of the wide, sloped window ledge;
if it slides in the rain and falls
on somebody's head, I'd probably
get sued.

There's something about Inwood that requires
a garden and its accompanying verse.
This finger of a neighborhood,
the Golan Heights of Manhattan, is wild
with trees and whalehump boulders that give
it mass as it seesaws on the island's
other end.

CARBON COPY

For Rose

This poem is to make the occasion
an event. Thirty-eight years of breath
is a lot of carbon. I thought to
figure the exact amount, but then
thought better.

Once, I wrote you birthday poems
to break the ice of daily life, each
one some sort of apology: Sorry
about rent and dishes and the common
madness. But my axe is dull, the warranty
expired, and under the ice, precisely,
is what?

And anyway, look: it splinters, melts, every
time our boy speaks or touches you
with heavy eyes, his dimples breach and
Splash! down you go warm and shivering
deep, deep.

I've gotten good at laundry, and poems
smell nothing like fresh laundry.
Poems reek of vapors, sweet and
gastric, bitter, skull miasmas, bloody
arrhythmias, and breath, of course, breath most
of all.

It's 13.87 metric tons, by the way, and
I thank you for all of it: your breath, in
exasperation, in mirth, in rage, in panting,
in sighs, in sleep, in words measured or idle
or wild, so much breath, like manna, wasted on
old me.

My body is given: what to do with him?—
So singular, so mine.

For the quiet joy of living, breathing,
Tell me, whom should I be thanking?

I am a gardener as I am a flower,
And in this darkhouse I am not alone.

Upon eternal panes already lie
My breathing and my warmth, my sigh—

A pattern, pressed upon the glass,
Unrecognizable as seconds pass.

So let the momentary murk drip soft,
For this dear pattern cannot be wiped off.

(1909)

When the mosaic grasses droop
And the resounding church is still,
Like a cunning snake, I drag myself
Through the dark to the foot of the cross.

I drink monastic tenderness
From concentrated hearts,
Like a hopeless cypress
On the deafened heights.

I love the curving brows,
The color on a saintly face,
The spots of gold and blood
That fleck the body of a waxen shape.

Maybe it's only the illusion of flesh
Deceiving us there in our dreams,
Flickering through their rags
And breathing fatal passions.

(1910)

THE LUTHERAN

I met a funeral Sunday, walking
by the Protestant kirk.
Passing absentminded, I noticed
stern and troubled faces.

Couldn't hear their foreign words,
nothing but a glint of bridle,
the empty Sunday street
a dull mirror for lazy horseshoes.

And in the elastic darkness of the carriage,
where sorrow hid, that hypocrite,
wordless, tearless, with nary a hello,
a glimpse of autumn roses in a buttonhole.

A black ribbon of foreigners,
tear-stained ladies walking
red-cheeked beneath veils, and stubborn
above them the coachman pushed on into the distance.

Whoever you were, departed Lutheran—
they buried you easily and simply.
Their eyes were blurred with measured tears,
the bells sounded restrained.

And I thought: Who needs eloquence?
We're no prophets, not even patriarchs.
We don't like heaven, and we're not afraid of hell.
In the gray of noon we burn, like candles.

(1912)

NOVGOROD

The wet smell of wooden churches, monks
that turn their backs like adolescent snobs.
Ivan the Terrible brought the Mongol yoke here,
frying the town fathers in a large well-seasoned wok.

As the chartered van prepares
for our return to Petersburg, a woman
runs to us through the rain.

Her arms are full of irises: "Kids,
I saw your van had Leningrad plates."

She's disappointed that we aren't real Petersburgers,
but the initial love is pushing at the awkward shock:

"My daughter is studying over there, so bring
these flowers to her city, it would lift my heart.
So what if you are Americans, with your films
frightening, but beautiful. And I like it
that your pensioners don't just sit around
drinking in their gardens, but travel the world

like youngsters."

CRYING MACHINES

Is it the mandolin?
Is it dead Scott Miller's
voice like tepid dog piss
trickling down the sidewalk?

"We Love You Carol and Alison"?
Who the fuck are Carol and Alison,
and why are they making me cry?

Tolstoy, help! "Music
makes me forget my real
situation. It transports me
into a state which is not my own.
Under the influence of music
I really seem to feel
what I do not feel, to understand
what I do not understand,
to have powers which I cannot have.
Music seems to me to act
like yawning or laughter."

Don't tell me what I think, Lev.
My real situation? I leak
because we are machines built
to store tears made by everything,

by the gum in your hair,
by the bluebells, bluebells,
by the lost Swiss Army knives,
by the ghost of Michael Furey,
by a dead girl and a bad handjob,
by the Sargasso stench, by the secrets
we forget or never knew
but remembered in the blood.

THE STALIN EPIGRAM

There's no ground for our legs but we're here,
Ten steps out and no words we can hear,
And when there's enough for a sliver of talk,
We'll surely mention the Kremlineer's walk.
His grubby fingers are greasy and fat,
His word drops like a kettlebell—and that's that.
His eyes are like cockroaches giggling and beaming,
And the rims of his boots are forever gleaming.

Amidst a gaggle of pencil-necked chieftains,
He plays the ivories of these quasi-humans.
This one tweets, that one meows, another whimpers,
While he alone prods and prattles and simpers.
He flings decrees like horseshoes, one, then another—
This one at the skull or the brow, in the eye or the bladder.
And if there's no execution today—then he'll razz the rest,
Preening and puffing his broad Ossete breast.

(1933)

EPIGRAM FOR DECEMBER 31, 2016

There's no ground for our legs....
—Osip Mandelstam

His words burst like mandarin grubs
in the mouth, the eyes, the nostrils, ears,

their juices sopped up by the hungry mobs:
it tastes like 1983 or 1953, like a chemical color
once banned, now restored.

The threat of threats, temptation of
temptations, nothing taken literally,
and everything is unknowable and
serious and

an afterschool cartoon joke:

If he says his name backwards surely
one of us will disappear.

PIGEON MILK, CONT'D

O pity a poor orphan
and the actor who plays him.
He's lost his script,
read him his lines.
He isn't pretending:
There is method in this,
adding and libbing, he will on
past the scene, parting
the orchestra, won't make

the parterre, he might even drown,
so quick, snap your fingers, coax him back
stageward with clapping and whistling,
hissing, and shout: bravo,
bravissimo, curtains for you.

AN EXTRAORDINARY ADVENTURE THAT HAPPENED TO VLADIMIR MAYAKOVSKY ONE SUMMER ON A DACHA

Sunset swarmed in a hundred forty suns,
as summer rolled into July;
there was the heat,
the swimming heat—
this all happened in the country.
The slopes of Pushkino, hump-backed
with Akulova Hill,
and below the hill—
there was a village
a crust of crooked roofs.
Beyond the village—
was a hole,
and in that hole, most likely,
the sun sank down each time,
so faithful, slowly.
But once again
tomorrow
to flood the world
the sun would rise up scarlet.
And day by day
this very thing
began
to make me
furious.
And one time so enraged was I
that all things paled in fear,
I shouted at the sun point-blank:
"Get over here!
Stop your loafing in that pitch-hole!
I shouted at the sun:
"Old sponger!
caressed by clouds you are,
while here—winter, summer,
I sit and draw these propaganda posters."

I shouted at the sun:
"Just you wait!
Listen here, goldenbrow,
instead
of setting aimlessly,
come by,
have tea with me!"
What have I done!
I'm dead!
Coming toward me
of his own good will,
the sun himself,
in wide beaming strides,
strode across the field.
Don't want to show I'm scared,
I saunter backwards, casual.
His eyes are in the garden now,
in windows,
doors,
through cracks, he came,
piled in, a sunny mass,
poured in;
and with a deep breath,
it spoke in basso:
"I drive the fires back
for the first time since creation.
You called me?
Boil some tea,
poet, spread out some jam, I say!"
Tears in my eyes—
out of my mind from the heat,
but I showed him
to the samovar and said:
"Well then, have a seat, you
luminary!"
Devil made me, raked my arrogance,
to shout at him like that, —
confused,
I sat on a bench corner,

scared—from frying pan to fire!
But, from the sun, a strange radiance
streamed, —
and formalities
forgotten,
I'm sitting, chatting
with the luminary freely.
I talk of this,
of that,
how I've been eaten alive by poster-work,
but the sun says:
"All right,
don't get fired up,
just look at things more simple!
Take me, you think it's
easy
shining on like this?
Go on and try it! —
You move along the sky—
since move you must,
you move—and shine your goddamn eyeballs out!"
We blabbed like that 'til it got dark—
'til what was night once, that is.
For what darkness was there here?
We were familiar with each other,
easy, free.
And soon, since friendship never melts,
I slap him hearty on the back.
And the sun does me the same:
"Me and you, comrade,
quite a pair we make!
Let's get out there, poet,
let's dawn
and sing
before this gray mess of a world.
I'll pour my sunny heart out,
and you—your own,
in verse."
A wall of shades,

a jail of nights
fell under the double-barreled suns.
A stir of rays and verse—
shine all you've got!
And if he gets tired,
and wants a night of rest,
dull sleepyhead,
that's when I
shine with all my might—
and day rings out again.
Shine all the time,
shine everywhere,
until the plunging end of days,
to shine—
to hell and back!
Here is my motto for you—
my slogan and the sun's!

(1920)

THE GERASIMOVS'

It was not my village:
sugar and egg yolk, liquid sun.
wild strawberries beaded
on a weed thread.

The log farmhouse hundreds
of years old, its timber cut down by axes
after the autumn rain to seal the grain
and left to cure until the spring,
not mine,

the palm-sized fish I caught in the pond
as a boy, my last summer in Russia,
salted and strung on the porch
to dry in the sun, not mine,

not then or now, the toasts to me and to my mother
and my wife and to the children we should have.

The past—near and distant—loses nothing
in the gentle beauty of what is not mine
to lose. Here, memory is born in seconds,
cut down by axes to seal the grain against
the moisture of all that is mine.

Not my village. I the one possessed.

OSIP MANDELSTAM (1891-1938) was one of the great Acmeist poets of Petersburg. His first two books, *Stone* (1913) and *Tristia* (1922), drew on the classical tradition of European civilization and, more specifically, on its architecture as a metaphor and guide for poetic practice itself—an idea Mandelstam would articulate in his essays. After settling in Moscow in 1922, Mandelstam shifted away from poetry toward memoir (*The Noise of Time*) and experimental fiction (*The Egyptian Stamp*), before returning to poetry in 1930 with *The Moscow Notebooks*. In 1934, he was arrested and sentenced to exile in the Russian provinces for reciting a blistering epigram attacking Stalin to a group of friends. While in exile he wrote *The Voronezh Notebooks*. Mandelstam was arrested again in 1938 for "anti-Soviet activities" and sentenced to hard labor. He died months later in a transit camp in Vladivostok.

VLADIMIR MAYAKOVSKY (1893-1930) was a brash poet, playwright, artist, and actor, who became a leading Russian Futurist. Having made his mark with such long poems as "The Backbone Flute" and "Cloud in Pants," he lent his talents to the Bolshevik Revolution, even as he began to chafe against the constraints of Soviet orthodoxy after completing two satirical plays (*The Bedbug* and *The Bathhouse*) lampooning government bureaucracy. He traveled to America in 1925 and to Western Europe in 1928. In 1935, five years after Mayakovsky took his own life in Moscow, Stalin praised his work, leading to his rehabilitation and canonization as the "Poet of the Revolution."

VAL VINOKUR (1972-) was born in Moscow and immigrated to Miami Beach as a child. He is the author of *The Trace of Judaism: Dostoevsky, Babel, Mandelstam, Levinas* (Northwestern 2009), and has published poetry, translations, and prose in *The Boston Review, New American Writing, The Literary Review, McSweeney's,* and *The Massachusetts Review*. His co-translations with Rose Réjouis were recognized with a Guggenheim Fellowship. He teaches literature at The New School, where he is chair of Liberal Arts in the BA Program for Adults and directs the minor in Literary Translation. His annotated translation of seventy-two stories by Isaac Babel, *The Essential Fictions*, was published in 2017. Vinokur is the founding editor of Poets & Traitors Press.